THE MALINOIS

FRANCOIS KIESGEN

FRANCOIS KIESGEN

Copyright © 2018 François Kiesgen
All rights reserved.

ISBN-13: 978-1986065337
ISBN-10: 1986065332

CONTENTS

1 WELCOME

2 ADVICE ON DOGS

3 THE MALINOIS

4 CHOOSING YOUR PUPPY

5 THE ARRIVAL OF THE PUPPY

6 THE PUPPY'S CLEANLINESS

7 THE PUPPY'S SOCIALIZATION

8 MY DOG

9 RULES OF EDUCATION

10 GAMES

11 EDUCATION

12 THE DOG'S CLEANLINESS

13 FOOD

14 SEXUALITY

1 WELCOME

You should know that by owning a puppy, you automatically support his raising mode. A puppy should be born and raised in accordance with his psychological and physiological needs. Narrowness and the bare minimum are not any puppy's needs. The puppy's parents have to be tested for predisposed illnesses. They should be registered at the LOF, because random one time intercourses will never guarantee the race specificities. The certified breeders guarantee the race continuity, it is their main duty. Your choice isn't that simple.

There are many approaches to raise your dog, the traditional one consists in punishment to make the dog understand when he behaves badly. This approach seems to have fast results but its basis is contested because it creates poor conditioning. The dog won't judge the situation or analyze the danger, he will react like a robot.

To raise a puppy, we suggest a method that uses positive reinforcement, and that profits from the Belgian Shepherd's Malinois intelligence, it is usually called "modern method".

2 ADVICE ON DOGS

The breeder's choice will be critical, because a good lineage will guarantee a dog that is compliant to the race's standard. The puppy is very sensitive, he won't be happy in a brutal or noisy climate, or in a hectic environment. He might become aggressive or fearful. Confidence is the key word in the relationship that you want to establish with your Belgian Shepherd Malinois. He absolutely needs attention and exercise, and if you can't procure these conditions, don't get a Belgian Shepherd Malinois, he will definitely be miserable.

Dogs have particularly ritualized behaviors, and that's what reigns on their reaction to our schedule and to their education. A dog is most comfortable and reassured with learnt and predictable rituels. .

The change of habits needs to be dealt with, and you need to prepare the dog using a progressive immersion if possible, and you should get closer to your dog in these moments. The situations that put stress on the dog lead to reactional behaviors, usually the development of hostility. He can be satisfied with a calm life of a pet dog if he gets the chance to have some training. Genetically, instinctively, dogs are programmed for actions. Dogs have emotions and feelings. We can't be sure of what our dog feels, but we can guess. This is not a mystery, observation is key.

The hierarchic mode is the universally common model. Every behavior of the dog is analyzed and interpreted into power and authority. There are dominant dogs and submissive dogs. Many dog trainers only aim to dominate their dog, and to break its character. That is similar to breaking the horse. It is an unhealthy obsession common with dogs. The idea to dominate the dog won't get you anywhere. The only way, the one that I've always used, is to communicate with the dog. The professionals, myself included, and those who work with professional dogs such as the Police, the Army or the National Security, are the best example. The dog gave us the authority so we can ensure his safety and his nutrition.

The master has to learn to interpret his dog's communication codes. The dog will also try to interpret its master's codes. The master who wants a Belgian Shepherd Malinois has to perfect and to maintain his relationship with his dogs. We will see that the dog tends to take initiatives according to precise codes. This is very important because a Belgian Shepherd Malinois learns fast, and obviously can't differentiate between a good and a bad behavior.

3 THE MALINOIS

The Belgian shepherd that has short tawny fur has been called Belgian shepherd dog of Mechlin for so long. This is the north western region of Belgium, called Brabant. The exact name of the town is Mechelen in Flemish, and it is located near Antwerp. The breed "Ter Heide" is the land of the Malinois.

This dog has the average size of a wolf, he has very short fur, and his color is fawn brindle. He was used in farming businesses as a guard for the farm and the herds. This is an intelligent dog. He has a pronounced instinct and a strong temperament. The moment he gets in your home, you have to fix rules and give him a sophisticated education. You should register him in the puppy school of the canine club of your region when he is 3 months old.

The Malinois imposed himself in Belgium over the other breeds with long fur: the short fur breed has a lot of qualities, and can be used in different roles. Today, the beauty qualities are important and the long fur is more frequently found in families whereas the short fur is often a professional.

The Malinois has exceptional qualities as a professional dog. But we can't say that there are breeds dedicated for work and others for family. The professional dogs come from a a draconian selection after individual tests. But genetically speaking, we won't necessarily have a professional dog when we cross selected dog breeds together. But this will ensure the persistence of the breed's features. It is completely wrong to sell a dog for high prices saying that he is a professional dog because this designation is only valid after the results of the selection tests. It is easier for a short fur dog to do some professional tasks. However, compared to the Groenendael and the Tervuren, the Malinois learns defending and guarding quicker because he was originally dedicated to guarding herds and farm, and that's why the selection of the aggressive dogs had started early on.

If he is socialized early enough, if he gets enough walks and is well educated, he can be an excellent family dog. However, he has character, and he needs a calm and patient master.

4 CHOOSING YOUR PUPPY

I will start by talking about you, future master, before giving you advice about choosing your Belgian Shepherd Malinois. The little ball of fur, it's cute, it's beautiful. Are you sure about your choice?

A dog means 12 to 14 years of common life with a companion.

Are you a player —not poker or Russian roulette- but ball or Frisbee. Playing is the secret to establish a camaraderie with your dog. If you associate playing and rewards, everything will be great. But be careful, the rewarding system is an art. You don't want to have a dog that is addicted to kibbles.

People will get mad at me, but a Belgian Shepherd Malinois can't be bought in a pet store, and especially not from an undeclared individual who has great puppies without LOF. Dog breeding is regulated. It is a business for professionals. We will have to negate a common idea once again. There is no such thing as a dominant dog. The dog is part of a pack, he will never be dominant or submissive, his behaviors will evolve according to the context and to his nature. But a dog can have some personality, he can be a little fearful or closed up. A test will help you understand the personality of the puppy, and education will play a big role.

A guard dog has to have character, be a little self-sufficient, independent even.

When you visit a dog farm for the first time, trust your gut, be observant, ask the breeder. With this book, you will learn many things. You will live ten to fourteen years with your companion. Come on, this is serious.

This is very private. Your kids will play with your Belgian Shepherd Malinois. Your dog has to be friendly. Be careful, with a kid, you cannot lose sight of the dog. Whatever the dog's race is, this rule is crucial.

To choose your puppy, there is a behavioral test elaborated by the psychologist William Campbell in the late Sixties and created to predict the behavioral tendencies of dogs that are subjected to people's orders and domination (physical and social).

Its purpose is to help a potential acquirer to choose the one that is most likely to adapt to the environment and to the family he will integrate.

The Campbell Test is very useful if we don't expect results other than the ones originally intended by this test: it's not an intelligence test, nor an aptitude test, and we can't expect it to provide indications in this direction.

In few cases, with races that have very specific personalities, like the Chow-Chow, the Campbell Test doesn't give reliable results.

The Test is done in forty to fifty days, and lasts half an hour. You will choose a calm and isolated location, closed, and with no distractions. It has to have an easily identifiable access. This location has to be foreign to the puppy.

The future owner of the puppy should ask to do the Test himself.

If the breeder tells you that he had already tested the pack, ask him kindly to allow you to redo the Test yourself. If he refuses, you will have to question the notoriety of the breeder.

You take the puppy that you are considering to a chosen location for the Test. This place is agreed upon with the breeder, of course.

You can't talk to the puppy, encourage him, or pet him. If the puppy does his business during the Test, ignore it, and clean the place when the puppy leaves.

<u>Social attraction:</u> place the puppy in the location's center and move away from him in the direction opposite to the access door. Crouch or sit cross-legged and clap gently to attract the puppy, he has to come to you.

<u>The attitude to follow:</u> stand next to the puppy, then move away from him while walking normally. The puppy has to follow you immediately.

<u>Response to a Constraint:</u> Crouch, turn the puppy on his back gently and keep him in this position for 30 seconds, your hand on his chest. The dog resists then calms down and licks you.

<u>Social dominance:</u> Crouch and pet the puppy gently, going from the head to the neck and back. The puppy turns his head and licks your hand.

<u>Dominance by Elevation:</u> take the puppy by entwining your fingers under its belly, palms facing up. Lift him slightly and keep him at that level for 30 seconds. The dog resists then calms down and licks your hands.

The complete Test is flexible according to the reactions. I've given you the best reactions you hope to get from the dog.

Some puppies have the tendency to react aggressively and could even bite. They won't fit in a family with children or old people, because they have too much personality and have to be raised by an informed owner who know how to deal with them.

Some puppies want to feel desired, without over doing it. They are not recommended in families who have little children or other dogs of the same sex.

Some puppies are extremely submissive, and should receive much kindness and gratification to fain some confidence and adapt in the human world. They will have trouble living with children.

You will have to judge the dog according to the Test. If the puppy responded the way I described, then he is well balanced and will be able to adapt everywhere, even if there are children or old people around. he has a high docility level.

5 THE ARRIVAL OF THE PUPPY

Before traveling, you have settled all the formalities, and you have been careful with the vaccinations. You have the health record, the origins booklet, the vaccination chart and the invoice.

For your journey, you should know that the Belgian Shepherd Malinois puppy is a frail being that will live a new experience that represents a big deal for it. You have to be understanding when dealing with your puppy.

You will take a pause every hour. You have some water, a dog bowl, some absorbent paper, two towels, and one of your old shirts.

Why, you ask? Well, the shirt will be of great use later because it will be permeated with your scent, and will become a marker for the dog.

When the Belgian Shepherd Malinois puppy enters the house, he has to find a corner ready for him. He should have a basket with a soft carpet. You should avoid wicker because the puppy will tear it up and swallow the pieces. You should provide two steel bowls and some toys. There should be two types of toys, some for fun and some for work.

Don't give your Belgian Shepherd Malinois plastic or foam toys because he will destroy them and swallow the pieces. I recommend a round ball, an oval ball and an elastomer stick. I am not sponsored, so I allow myself to recommend the brand Kong, which I think is the more resistant. Moreover, the toy contains a treat for the dog. The dog's weight will have an effect on his non-protected articulations, which with time will cause calcites in his paws and knees. Give your puppy a comfortable pillow and a washable sheet, if possible.

You should not give these toys immediately to the Belgian Shepherd Malinois puppy. You should wait at least three days before playing with him. And then, you can give them to the puppy.

The work toys should be kept for the puppy's coaching. This process is the basis of the Belgian Shepherd Malinois puppy's education.

When he arrives, the dog should get used to his new home and to his new family. Be patient, allow the puppy to establish his markers. You should wait for your dog to feel safe and protected before you start soliciting him.

At his arrival, keep on with the cuddles, and let the puppy explore his new home. At that time, he may have an urgent need and you should pretend it didn't happen. Please, do not show the dog that you are cleaning, do not mark the moment of his needs. That may extend the house training time for the puppy.

If you have a garden, you can anticipate the moment of the urgent need. Your Belgian Shepherd Malinois puppy will be house trained quickly.

The puppy will stick his muzzle everywhere. Let him do as he wishes, that will allow him to become familiar with the environment. At one point, he will do something wrong, and your first education lesson will start.

You should know how to say "NO" firmly. This is very important.

Don't worry if you have to repeat your words. During the first two weeks, you will just have to repeat the word "NO" as many times as needed. There should be no punishment.

Do not rush to the dog every time he whines, he may learn that bad behavior.

The dog lives his life, and you live yours. It's not the dog that decides.

Prevent any accident by learning to lift the puppy properly, put a hand on his chest, and the other one under his behind.

After a week, you will only have to say "NO" two times. If the dog continues, do not insist. You will have to change strategies. First lesson: you shouldn't yell. Second lesson: you should never touch the dog to constrain him.

You should associate the order "NO" to a sound. I use a plastic water bottle filled with pebbles. You will throw the bottle to the right or the left of the dog while saying the order "NO" sharply.

I say to the right or the left, and far enough from him. It is just a mean to distract him. You should be careful not to hit the dog with the bottle, because he will become fearful.

Please keep in mind that this is not a toy, but an education tool, so don't give the bottle to the dog.

The puppy should stay a week in his home with his family. He shouldn't stay alone because he will feel stressed and disoriented. And your puppy will respond to his imbalance the way he sees fit. There is the matter of house training, of course. Do you think the dog will do it outside? You can try. But do not expose the puppy too much because he doesn't have an immune system at that age.

After a week, go out and leave the puppy alone at home for five minutes, then come back inside. Compliment him, he behaved well, he will be happy to see you. If he did his business, or a mistake, pretend it didn't happen. You could limit the time, and redo the test with three minutes. Usually we start with five minutes, then ten. Do it every day, and increase the time. The dog doesn't have a sense of time. But he is afraid of being abandoned. So, you should transform the abandonment thought to a positive wait.

Later, you will leave your house to your dog. So don't miss the first basis of education.

After the first two weeks at your home, the dog should go out, and there is a process to respect. For his first time out, the dog will wear a leash and a leather collar. Do not buy a choker collar or an electronic one.

Now you master the first command, which is the "NO". You need to work on the order "WALK". You should go to a calm place and teach your Belgian Shepherd Malinois puppy to walk beside you. Start by placing your dog on your left, then command "name of your dog – WALK" and move your left leg. The carabiner has to fall freely; the puppy's shoulders have to be at the level of your knees. The puppy has to follow you, not to outpace you. Be gentle, you are not correcting the puppy, you are teaching him. Don't worry, he understands. The dog is a learning process. Be comprehensive. Did you learn immediately?

At the beginning, you should only teach him to walk on a leash. Your command should always be "name of your dog – WALK" and you place the puppy in the correct position. I've said be gentle, because he is a puppy. However, he has the right to go out, and he shouldn't learn a wrong behavior. Do not skip steps. You have surely noticed that we started his education early on.

The outings should have progressive duration and complexity. Do not expose your Belgian Shepherd Malinois puppy to the jam of rush hours.

Start with walks in the countryside, then in the city (in a location that is protected and closed), then you can slowly expose the Belgian Shepherd Malinois puppy.

Sooner or later, your Belgian Shepherd Malinois puppy will be scared. Please, do not mark this behavior. Act as if you haven't noticed and keep on walking. You should never congratulate your puppy for a wrong behavior.

This is the summary of my teaching method with a Belgian Shepherd Malinois puppy: the marking and the positive reinforcement. Nothing else.

When we want some tranquility in the house, we can use a paddock for the puppy. The dog should have a landmark, his basket. He should get used to going there. It's his place, you can't go there.

You can have a metallic transport cage. He must get used to it early on.

To get the Belgian Shepherd Malinois puppy to use his basket, then to accept his transport cage, you should begin by placing there a chewing bone, his favorite toy and especially the shirt that was used when the dog arrived, that carries your scent. The olfactory marking is a way to reassure the dog. The puppy should never be bothered when he is in his place.

6 THE PUPPY'S CLEANLINESS

For your Belgian Shepherd Malinois puppy, cleanliness means not doing it on his sleeping and feeding place. The puppy has to learn new meanings to the word cleanliness. To facilitate the learning process, you should respect some rules.
Feed him at fixed hours, not late at nights if possible.
Let the dog eat alone calmly, then take away his bowl after twenty minutes, whether it is empty or not.
The dog should always have access to clean water.
Knowing that the dog has needs after meals, take him out after he's eaten, but don't make him run.
A puppy sleeps a lot, he will rest for many hours, and will want to do it almost immediately after he wakes up. Take him out immediately after his nap.
An 8-weeks-old puppy can't hold it for more than one or two hours during the day, and 3 or 4 hours during the night, so be patient. You can count the hours and take the puppy out. I can assure you that it works perfectly, if you take out the dog after meals, naps, playing sessions, at night before bed and in the first hours of morning. A Belgian Shepherd Malinois will understand quickly, and will learn to

come alert you.

You can't expect the Belgian Shepherd Malinois puppy to hold it for many hours before he's at least 6 months old.

You have to take the puppy out at least three times a day.

The puppy will sometimes do it at home, do not punish him. But do not mark this wrong behavior. Act like it didn't happen.

It is obvious that you need to take out the Belgian Shepherd Malinois puppy often and since a young age.

At first, you should calk him on leash in clean and calm places.

The populated and noisy areas are prohibited.

You should take the Belgian Shepherd Malinois puppy out before he's 3 months old. The risk of infections is minor. But it is great for its education. He will quickly become well-balanced and able to do it on leash wherever you go. And even if you have a garden, you still should take you Belgian Shepherd Malinois puppy to the countryside.

Finally, do not fixate on the cleanliness matter, it will be perfected in six to eight months.

7 THE PUPPY'S SOCIALIZATION

When he's eight weeks old, the Belgian Shepherd Malinois puppy is legally allowed to leave the place in which he was born.

He has to discover his new 'home' and keep learning the basics of life.

The Belgian Shepherd Malinois puppy needs new experiences to acquire a satisfactory behavioral balance. This confrontation with the world has to happen within good conditions (no anxiety factors allowed).

The puppy has grown with his mother, and she had to instill some rules into him. Best case scenario, he also had brothers and sisters and interacted with them, played with them and learnt to share with them. If he used to live in the countryside and finds himself living in the city —and vice versa- this is a first big change in his life.

New noises and a new environment are a lot to take in at first! That's why he should be welcomed in a calm location.

A week after his arrival, the Belgian Shepherd Malinois puppy should be handled regularly but carefully, and progressively confronted to the different noises of daily life. He will quickly feel comfortable with these changes.

Next, he has to be confronted to the noises of TV, radio, vacuum, broom, the neighbors, the garden, and the visitors. As soon as the puppy receives his vaccinations, you can take him out without fearing for his health. This is crucial. Get him progressively used to all the noises, and all the places. These little immersions at a young age will help prevent many problems later in life. And above all, let him meet people. Stop, shake hands with them, and get him used to the kids that see him on the street and want to pet him.

There is another received idea that should be discarded: to preserve his guardian instinct, the dog should never be petted by strangers. This is completely false. The dog should be socialized. If not, he won't be a good watchdog, he will become a caged lion ready to jump on anything that moves.

The Belgian Shepherd Malinois puppy should meet kids of different ages. If you don't have kids in your home, you should find kids for your dog to play with. However, there should always be an adult around to supervise them. Their games should never become too heated, and you have to ensure that this is a positive experience for the dog.

The Belgian Shepherd Malinois puppy should be around adult dogs. If the puppy hurts the adult, the latter will find a way to stop the little one, either with a roar or with a bark. Stop your puppy immediately. These tips are crucial for his education. Teach your puppy to accept being manipulated by other people at a young age. Ask your friends to gently touch his ears, eyes, tail, gums and teeth.

Give your puppy a little treat for having allowed this socialization. However, you have to be the only one treating the puppy. Try to remember this rule. Don't allow anyone to feed your Belgian Shepherd Malinois puppy, this is the basis of the bait refusal education. This way, the puppy will learn that being manipulated by many people is an enjoyable experience, and that he can only eat what his master gives him. If you will use day-care services, the dog should be introduced to the host and progressively immersed (an hour in day-care, then two…), don't put your puppy in day-care until his education is complete, at eighteen months. If you use your dog as a watchdog, avoid day-care services and leave your dog with known relatives.

8 MY DOG

The puppy moves, plays, and communicates. It is very important that his master offers him walks, toys and interactions.

You should know that between the ages of twelve to fourteen months, the dog will certainly experience an adolescence crisis, and will want to stand up to his master. You have to stay calm, firm, and keep interacting. This phase lasts two or three months.

Heat moments will require attention whether your dog is male or female. It is important to chose a contraceptive method (definitive or reversible depending on your future vision).

Most caninc bchavioral problems are caused by an education excessively harsh or excessively soft. The dog doesn't like the tranquility of a repetitive schedule, he prefers to participate in the family life or to interact with his master or educator. In consequence, the dog needs to be exposed to different situations. This is important because an uneducated dog will present a problem.

A harsh education will make the dog fearful. The dog should have absolute trust in his master, and he is naturally fearful at the start. If you break this trust, the relationship will be irrevocably destroyed. This type of education can also result in an aggressive and dangerous dog. A soft education will result in a whiny dog that barks all the time to get your attention.

Dogs are intelligent, and you need to invest in a good education.

9 RULES OF EDUCATION

You should never touch a Belgian Shepherd Malinois in order to constraint him. When I say touch, I mean wanting to impose a posture onto him. We will never use an electronic leash or a choker one. You are not punishing the dog, this is highly unhealthy and violent, you should only say "NO" firmly. I recommend using a professional harness. This is easier for the dog and less dangerous to his neck. You should never yell. The dog feels the ultrasound, so he can hear you even if you talk in a low voice. The voice modulation will be your pedagogic tool. You have to force yourself to talk normally to your Belgian Shepherd Malinois. You can only use a yelled order in extremely urgent cases, and that will be the center of a specific education. If you waste all your bullets now you will be disarmed in an extreme situation. I recommend you to talk in a low voice, to repeat while raising your voice lightly, and nothing else. Obviously, the dog can disobey you, even rebel, but we have other tactics. If you associate the voice, a gesture and a sound. Learn to 'pout' and to turn your head away from your Belgian Shepherd Malinois if he doesn't listen to you. I don't love you anymore and I won't take care of you, he hates this strategy. Even a registered guard dog Belgian Shepherd Malinois with many interventions. I can confirm this. Remember that I respond to the dog's bad behavior with a proportional action (voice, gesture, and pout), then I cancel the punishment after two minutes.

Some people say that it's not possible, that you need to yell, to punish, to lock, to hit… Do not listen to them… They never had to deal with an agitated Belgian Shepherd Malinois. They are ignorant and irresponsible. And that's a shame because their dog will never act upon his instincts and he will be dependent and even fearful of his master: That's the worst possible scenario. The puppy and the dog are two different realities, and we have to talk about 'teaching' a puppy and 'educating' a dog. Do not use the word 'train'. Did they train you when you were a kid? When he is young, the puppy has a very different psychology. The puppy reacts to stimulations differently from a dog. You have to understand that the mental structures of a young puppy is like a sponge ready to absorb tons of information. A puppy shouldn't work more than half an hour during the first six months, then you can increase the effort. You have to start educating the puppy early. But you have to respect this rule, you have to work often, but not a lot. The 'work' for puppies is based on playing and pleasure. You can also learn to modulate the tone of your voice like professionals, and use a normal voice for all the daily orders, and raise your voice for more complex orders and sequences. The first rule is to reward an expected behavior, and to act like the inadequate behavior didn't happen. The second rule is that you have to teach, make him repeat, then associate the expected behaviors. The crucial rule is that the learning process is always based on playing and treats.

In conclusion, the education process is based on playing,

the association is done with repetition and teaching, the integration of behavior sequences is done with routine. Above all, the rewarding is the sharing of joy between the master and the dog.

10 GAMES

When you are playing with your Belgian Shepherd Malinois puppy, everybody has to win. And the master never loses, this is a crucial rule.

What matters is to use games to teach. An awarded behavior should be repeated, and a behavior reprimanded by a 'NO' will decrease in frequency and may even disappear.

Positive reinforcement is the basis of education via games. To win and to lose increase your perseverance, so you persist and you get better, and one day you become a champion. But you have to win sometimes or else you will be frustrated and you will give up. You have to let your Belgian Shepherd Malinois win, and that will boost his motivation. This is important for a Belgian Shepherd Malinois.

Traction games are harmless. They derive from the disputes over a prey. The dog loves this game. This is a game that reinforces the intensity of the dog's jaw clutching. If the dog tries to bite you, the traction game is immediately stopped.

Fetch games are recommended for dogs. You throw a ball. The dog has to run to the place where the ball fell. Then, you will teach him to get you the ball back, to give it to you, and to got fetch it if you throw it again. If the dog gets angry, stop the game immediately.

In aquatic environment, you should use a floating ring instead of a ball for the fetch game. The dog loves playing in the water. Do not deprive him of this pleasure, he can swim.

11 EDUCATION

Walking on leash

When a dog pulls on his leash, he gets in front to sniff a particularly appreciated place, join a play mate, do something that he likes. The master has to refuse. If not, pulling on the leash will be awarded by the realization of the goal. You have to resist and be firm so that your companion walks with you on leash. You have to stop if the dog pulls on his leash, then wait a little and give the order 'no'. You shouldn't block the dog with our leg to force him to get back. With dogs, you should change directions when you feel that he is pulling, stop and say 'no'.

Sit, lie down, up

A treat helps teach the dog to sit, lie down, and get up.
At first, you say the order when the dog gets in the desired position then you do an adequate gesture, like raising a hand for the 'up', lowering it for the 'lie down' and keeping it horizontal for the 'sit'. You should also associate a clicker sound, for example: one bang for the order 'sit', two bangs

for the order 'lie down', one long bang for the 'up'. You finish every exercise with a signal (for example: go play). Never forget the treat (after every exercise for the puppy, after every session for the dog). You should always pet the dog immediately after he executes an order correctly.

Work on the order 'sit'

Take a treat in your hand and hold it so that the dog can smell it and lick it without being able to eat it. You will move the treat slowly from his muzzle to above his head. the dog will start sitting so that he can be comfortable while following the treat with his eyes. Now, you follow the movement with the order, the gesture and the sound. As soon as his behind touches the ground, give him the treat. You can teach him using the order first, then the order and the gesture, and finally the order, the gesture and the sound, but I don't recommend this method. This is less adapted to the dog's conditioning.
With a Belgian Shepherd Malinois, you have to work on the three acknowledgment systems. With three different signals, you will not confuse him, which is very important for the orders 'stop' and 'come'.

Work on the order 'lie down'

You shouldn't work starting from the sitting position, this will hinder the conditioning. You should start from the 'up' order. You move the treat from his muzzle down to the floor. The dog will follow your movement. You can only give him the treat when he is lying down. You can place a treat under a chair or a table to force the dog to lie down to eat it.

Keep in mind that at first, you shouldn't give the order when the dog is getting ready to take the desired position.

Work on the order 'up'

The dog is lying down, hold a treat next to his muzzle and move it away slowly making a line parallel to the floor. When the dog lifts his paws to get up, give him the treat.

Work on the order 'Don't move'

Start from the position 'sit', hold a treat in your hand, wait until the dog starts to move, give the order 'don't move' and give the treat.

In time, your dog will gain in confidence and will respect the position 'don't move' longer. Then, you will have to do the exercise while moving away progressively from your Belgian Shepherd Malinois.

Start with a distance of 1 meter, then you will give the order and reward the dog. Before increasing the distance you have to be sure that the dog doesn't move during the exercise. After that, you will have to hide and leave the dog in position with the order 'don't move'.

You shouldn't look for the failures, you have to patiently anchor the distances in order to make him accept longer ones.

Distance Working on the basic positions

The dog has to learn that he doesn't need to be near you for the order to be active, but that he has to take the position wherever he is, the moment you ask him to. The coordination of the word, gesture and sound is essential.

Attach your dog to a tree and move away from him for 2 m and order him 'sit'. Join the dog and award him. You will increase the distance progressively. If needed, you will get back to the previous distance. Before increasing the distance you have to be sure that the dog doesn't move during the exercise. You shouldn't look for failures, you have to patiently anchor the distances in order to make him accept longer ones. Now, you redo the work with the dog on leash (it has to be a closed location).

In distance working on the basic positions, we include the finish signal 'stop'.

You walk, then you give your Belgian Shepherd Malinois the order 'sit' then the order 'don't move' and you take two steps then you give the order 'come'. You should increase the distance progressively. In a different exercise, you will ask your dog to stay 'up' and you will keep on walking while giving the order 'don't move'. Never forget to congratulate and to award. As you keep doing the exercise, you should keep congratulating him, but the award is only given when the session is over.

Walk: The order 'walk' is important, you worked on it before but we still have to anchor it. In many situations, when you walk with the dog, this will be a mean to call back the dog and to get him used to walking beside you. You need to teach your dog to walk on your right side. In town, the dog has to walk away from the traffic.

As for walking without leash, you need to start walking on leash, and then take it off while keeping a hand on the dog's back. Give him a treat. Now, you give the order 'walk', the dog follows you. You give him a treat every 10 meters, then you space treats. You should increase the time during which the dog walks beside you without leash progressively. To keep the dog concentrated, you should give the order 'walk' regularly.

You have to be patient, you absolutely need the dog to collaborate with you. If you do this exercise with the leash on, there is a high probability that you will never be able to let the dog walk without his leash.

The order 'walk' has to be worked on during every outing. When you start walking, when you decide to take off the leash, you will give the order 'walk' many times. The award is to let the dog walk freely. Of course, the dog has to be controlled especially if there is a visibility problem, or if there is a risk of coming across other dog-walkers. The rule is to let the dog walk beside you and put the leash on when you come across lot of people with or without dog. If the dog doesn't listen to your 'walk' order he has to be put on leash immediately, for about 10 minutes. After this duration, you will test him again, and if the dog disobeys again, the rest of the walk will be done on leash.

The order 'no'

'No' is an order that means 'You can give up now, I forbid it'. If you want to have a well-educated dog, you need to spend time on this order. Obviously, you a, choose a different word, the important thing is to associate a gesture and a sound to it. You need to avoid confusing the dog with a gesture and a sound similar to another order.

For the first exercise, hold a treat, hold your dog on leash, allow the dog to see and to smell the treat without being able to get to it. When the dog pulls on his leash to try getting the treat, give the order 'no' one time. And then, be quiet. At that moment, will the dog try to disobey? You absolutely need to stay in place and to hold your ground: be quiet and turn your head. the dog will want to disobey. The temptation will increase and the exercise will become interesting. You have to repeat the order 'no' after a minute. Then you will increase the time.

During your outings, you need to periodically verify if the dog understands the meaning of the order 'no'. during his education, the order 'no' means interdiction. There are direct interdictions and interdictions that need to be embedded in the dog's mind even in your absence, like bait refusal. This is easy to teach.

Before the outing, you will place on the road several treaties under rocks, so that the dog can see it. And then, you will use the order 'no'. the dog will react better to the order 'no' if you train him a lot. Be careful though: do not use the order if the dog has already touched the food. In that case, reprimand him using a firm voice 'NO', leave him on leash and do not talk to him for ten minutes.

The order 'give':

Teaching a Belgian Shepherd Malinois to give an object under your order will be beneficial and indispensable in an urgent context. This exercise is based on exchange, not obligation. You will need some wooden weights, on one hand because that's the object used in canine sports and on the other hand because the dog can't swallow this type of objects. In the beginning of the education process, you will use a ball in which you will put a treat. You throw the ball. You give the order 'go get'. The dog can't take the treat, he will get you the ball. You give the order 'give' and you offer him a treat. The most important thing is to not skip steps, and to do the exercise one or two times.

Recall:

An ordered dog that turns around without hesitation when

he is highly distracted by the environment and that comes back quickly to his master has great recall instinct. You can let go of your dog only under these conditions. The basic rule of recall is to only recall the dog when you are sure he will come to you. To get this result with a Belgian Shepherd Malinois, you have to start by teaching him the order 'walk' and give that order when the dog is less than 2 m away from you. The recall has to leave no room for thought for the dog, it has to induce an immediate reaction. You shouldn't wait long to see if your dog will obey you. You have to repeat it every day, and know that this routine is never taken for granted. During the outings, you have to test your dog. If the outcome is negative, put the leash on. A Belgian Shepherd Malinois will respect the code: freedom in exchange of immediate recall.

The secret of recall is to work daily and to have three signals (for example a whistle, a hand gesture and the order 'walk'). Your dog must know exactly what the order 'walk' means.

The order 'stop':

The order 'stop' and the order 'walk' have to be practiced separately. The order 'walk' concerns the recall. The order 'stop' is a request of immediate stop in case of emergency, where the dog stops wherever he is. The order 'stop' must be practiced once the dog masters the order 'walk'. During an outing, you change directions and you observe your dog and you give the order 'stop'.

The recall and the stop should be practiced on every outing and many times during each outing. You shouldn't give many orders at a time, but you should integrate them to the dog's daily life. You will progressively notice that the dog comes back quickly, he's in the game, and you should award him because you have won and the confidence bond is established.

The 'zero risk' doesn't exist, there will always be disobediences, even for a dog like yours. When dogs meet, the best way to solve a tricky situations s to keep walking quickly and nonchalantly. If you stay in place, you are creating a possible fight. If the dogs get in a fight, the two owners should get away from each other in opposite directions; this is the easiest method to make an end to the hostility. This option is only possible when the two owners are aware of the disobedience of their animals.

The crucial rule: a dog that provokes another one is immediately stopped by his master.

12 THE DOG'S CLEANLINESS

Even if the dog is strong and is healthy, he can still develop diseases. We don't know if there are any illnesses specific to the Belgian Shepherd Malinois in addition to those that touch all big dogs.

The dog that has short fur doesn't need elaborate grooming sessions. A regular brushing in order to eliminate the dead hair is enough. During the molting period, a more thorough grooming might be needed. On the other hand, long fur needs daily brushing.

His ears and eyes don't need special care, but still need cleaning once in a while.

The dog needs to explore many territories. Whether he lives in an apartment or in a house, he can't be satisfied with a simple outing of 10 minutes or with a small garden. He needs regular outings.

Ears: you need to check the property of your dog's ears regularly. If needed, you need to clean then with an appropriate lotion (you will find them at your vet's, in drug stores or in pet stores) using cotton or a tissue. Never use cotton swabs, you could injure your dog if he moves abruptly, and it is not a good way to clean his ears anyway.

Eyes: clean them regularly using a special lotion. Every abnormal flow should immediately be checked by your vet.

Teeth: Keep an eye on the scaling in his teeth. Scale can cause many serious problems like early receding gums, bad breath, dental abscess…

During your dog's growth check his dentition regularly: his milk teeth will fall when he is 4 months old. This process can go unnoticed because he will swallow most of them. If you have doubts concerning your puppy's teeth changing, check your vet.

Claws: Normally they will wear out regularly due to the hard floors.

Bath: you can bathe your puppy 8 days after his first booster vaccination. You should always use a dog shampoo (pet stores and drug stores) and dry him well (be careful when using a hair dryer because it can burn his skin if you put it too close to him). Ideally, the water should be warm. Do not overdo it with baths.

Many people think that shepherds are more susceptible to develop hip dysplasia. In reality, this genetic malformation can affect almost every dog of medium to big size. Hip dysplasia is a malformation or deformation caused by the abnormal development of a tissue or an organ.

Today, the best breeders only use non-affected dogs and A-classed dogs for reproduction. X-rays are done on adult dogs for prevention purposes. If the dog is affected, he won't be a breeder. You need to pay attention to another affection; gastric dilatation volvulus, the torsion of the stomach. This can happen if the dog makes an effort after having eaten. I am not a fan of feeding late at night, before bed. But this can be a solution.

I feed my dogs early in the morning and I wait for digestion.

You should give your dog flea and tick treatment during hot seasons, and a deworming twice a year. Do not forget the yearly vet visit for the vaccination boost.

The health record and medical monitoring are mandatory. Depending on the region and the risks, your vet will advice you. Other vaccines and protections may be necessary in some regions.

To respect the dog's nutritional needs, it is recommended to give the dog good quality kibbles. If possible, ask your vet about the best possible nutrition.

To take care of your dog, you need to acquire scissors, tweezers, anti-venom syringes, claw clippers, braces, and a telescopic rod. Do not forget that you are not a vet. You should have some medicines at home for first aid care.

You need: gauze, disinfectant, plaster, band aids, soap, physiologic serum for eye care, antibiotic cream for cuts, ether for ticks, intestinal medicine for diarrhea. If you are going on a trip, you need to add: antibiotics to prevent allergies, anti-vomiting, flea protection, deworming, scabies treatment for ears and anti-chiggers cream.

You can also form a medical pharmacy for first aid care, but you should always check a vet in case of persistent symptoms. These are the products to use for each affection.

For skin problems, there are antiseptics: alcohol, betadine, iodized alcohol, methylene blue, oxygenated water, ether or Dakin.

Be careful; these products are usually irritating when used as pure solutions. The dilution depends on the product and on its punctual use. Marseille soap is the simplest and most effective antiseptic when used correctly, and it can be used on different cuts.

An infected cut must be soaped, rinsed abundantly. Then,

we apply antiseptics, alcohol or tincture of iodine. Oxygenated water is very effective in cleaning a cut. It removes any trace of blood. Antibiotic sprays are used to prevent localized infections.

For the other skin problems, you will need a scabies treatment based on Lindane, an anti-mycosis product for ringworms, spray or pills. An anti-inflammatory lotion will allow you to treat allergies and eczema.

For digestive problems, you should know that diarrhea is frequent. Your pharmacy should contain a gastric protector, in the form of powder or gel. An antispasmodic to regulate bowel movements. An antibiotic that acts against digestive germs. For constipation, you should use paraffin oil.

For infections, antibiotics are mandatory. But you should always use them on prescription. Check with your vet and explain to him that you travel a lot even on the week end and that it won't be easy to find animal emergency rooms in certain places. You will establish a list of antibiotics with your vet, according to your dog.

It is crucial to choose a good breeder that avoids consanguinity, practices a rigorous selection of breeders, and that will give you the reports of the hip X-rays of the breeders.

13 FOOD

Like great athletes, the dog needs an adequate nutrition. When he is exercising or competing in a contest, the dog has greater needs in proteins and carbohydrates. Proteins allow him to make big efforts whereas carbohydrates allow him to exercise for long durations.

Apart from activity periods, the dog can be given industrial nutrition, dry or wet. The dog should always have a bowl of fresh water.

His nutrition should be of good quality, highly digestible, and divided into two fractions if possible. Big dogs can experience gastric dilatation volvulus, so you should avoid big rations and efforts or stress right before or after a meal.

For a professional dog, you should pay particular attention to his articulations. Before practicing sports, he should have a good warm-up. He is ambitious and energetic, he has trouble saving his energy, so you have to do it for him. **This is very important especially during his growth, so you should avoid excessive activities.**

To have a healthy dog, you should focus on the quality of his nutrition.

At first, you should feed your dog twice a day. If the meal

is not finished in twenty minutes, take away his bowl and don't allow him to eat between meals.

Never allow your dog to get his muzzle to the level of your plate (hygiene), or to steal food from the table: sanction him if you catch him in the act by talking to him in a firm voice '**NO'.**

Many dogs may have weight problems. You have to incorporate a healthy diet to his lifestyle. I own four dogs and I have four types of kibbles. Twice a week, I give some fresh ones. But all this is personal.

Industrial nutrition provide dog owners with nutrients adapted to the weight, height and age of the dog. It also provides nutrients that match the level of activity of each dog.

The dog's ration should always be given at the same time and at the same place. The dog should eat alone in a quiet place at home, always near his masters.

Water is very important, and should always be available. If he drinks too much, you should check your vet.

There are three types of nutrition; dry industrial nutrition, wet industrial nutrition and 'home' nutrition. We will describe each one of these types and detail their pros and cons.

You should know though that you can't abruptly change the nutrition of a dog.

It is agreed that the dog will be given two types of food during a period of 8 days.

The dry nutrition is based on kibbles. The kibble is made of dough, rice, meat, fish, and vegetables. It is a dehydrated food that needs a great water consumption. There are different kibbles for all types of dogs, according to their morphology. At the back of the box you will find the exact ration that you should give your dog daily. These kibbles provide the daily energetic needs of an active adult dog. They ensure a healthy and balanced nutrition for the dog by giving him nutrients prepared by nutritionists and specialized veterinaries.

Some dogs do not like kibbles and refuse to eat them because they don't find them appetizing. If your dog has tasted another type of food, it is possible that he will abandon his bowl and ask for his favorite food. You can mix kibbles with meat or with wet industrial food in order to better their taste.

Kibbles are usually a great way to fight tartar deposit thanks to their abrasive properties. They are recommended by breeders and vets.

Nutrition based on raw meat is equally called BARF, as in "Biologically Appropriate Raw Food". The diet BARF is a natural approach to the dog's nutrition. The food choice is based on respecting the animal's specific physiology. The dog is a carnivorous animal, so it is only natural to offer him a carnivore nutrition based on meat, raw bones and offal. This diet relies heavily on the idea that the alimentary choices of wild animals are guided by their biological needs. In the wilderness, animals instinctively choose the most appropriate diet to their metabolism. However, pet carnivores can't do that anymore because their owner is the one that gives them their daily needs.

The wet industrial nutrition is the food contained in the 'cans' found at every grocery store. The daily needs of an active adult dog are provided by this type of food. The can's packaging is prepared by canine nutrition specialists that ensure a healthy and balances nutrition for the dog. These cans have to be preserved in the fridge to avoid food intoxication. The can's price is twice as much as the kibbles price.

The 'home' nutrition is the food that you prepare yourself. You absolutely have to give your dog some fresh ingredients. The owner certainly loves his animal, but the food he prepares for him usually lacks in minerals and vitamins. Contrary to kibbles and cans, the quality of the food is a real problem because the owner usually gives his dog a different quantity every day, which can cause obesity.

Animals, like people, need a healthy and balanced nutrition for their well-being. Contrary to popular beliefs, this type of nutrition is more expensive than industrial nutrition, and needs particular care.

Why do some dogs seem difficult, refuse the food that their master gives them while other dogs swallow everything in a second? Like human beings, we can find dogs that eat a lot and dogs that eat a little. This attraction to food seems attached in part to genetic causes. We also know that the period between weaning and the age of three months is a delicate phase in which puppies are highly influenced and learn to choose what to eat and what not to eat.

This adaptation process prevents the animal from swallowing things that may cause him harm. This may explain why a dog sometimes refuses a type of food that he has never tasted when young.

In conclusion, kibbles are better than wet food because the latter has many pejorative aspects, especially on the dog's teeth. In addition, it is very difficult to cook a meal that perfectly respects the nutritional needs of the dog. The food should never be given at any time, randomly. In fact, the food excess can cause digestive problems and obesity.

It is also forbidden to give mineral supplements to a puppy that gets a balanced diet. That may harm him and cause bone malformations. Final, it is unnecessary and even harmful to diversify your puppy's nutrition.

But if a change is necessary, you have to do it progressively or else the puppy will experience gastro intestinal problems. When faced with a sudden and prolonged food refusal, and I'm not talking about a short-lived behavior, you should check with your vet.

If there is no illness diagnosed, you have to look for another reason. The dog is a sensitive creature. A change of environment, the loss of a human or animal companion can make him refuse food for a couple of days. I advise you to respect this diet and not to panic. If this trend persists, you should check with the vet again, and insist.

Some dogs eat non edible stuff like dirt, rocks, wood, plastic, pottery, even socks, etc... Some of this stuff was also found in the stomachs of Italian wolves in the beginning of the XXth century.

This behavior, called Pica, seems influenced by genetic causes because it is seen in some species more than others. These subjects do not suffer of nutritional deficits.

The dog can act that way for different reasons: boredom, big changes, grief. Sometimes, he does it to attract his master's attention.

If your dog swallows poop, whether his poop or other dogs' poop, it is because he finds it appetizing; especially when it contains partially digested food. Only say 'NO' firmly.

If the dog swallows his own poop, this may be because the dog was severely punished in the past for having pooped in the house. In this case, the master has certainly forgotten the first rule of the chapter education "Pretend it didn't happen".

How do we make them stop these unhealthy habits? You can sprinkle the stuff he likes to swallow with a strong substance (like paprika). Distract him by throwing a bottle containing rocks or by making noise, and don't forget to award him if he stops.

But if your dog gnaws at wood and ingests non digestible fibers, this is no big deal.

Concerning obesity, some studies show that in most cases, obesity is related to bad nutritional habits and low quality food.

The obese dog shouldn't be anthropomorphized: no human feelings. We decrease the quantities, we switch to obese dog kibbles, we exercise more. Eventually, we can associate diets.

The pleasure of eating comes from a subjective and personal perception of flavor. The tasting process happens in the taste buds; little protrusions located in the posterior part of the tongue which contain sensorial cells. These cells react to different chemical substances and transmit the received information to the brain's neurons. The dog has less taste buds than human beings (about 2000 in dogs and 10000 in human beings). Although they can differentiate between sweet, salty, acid and bitter tastes, this process is much less precise. That's why our dogs aren't big gourmets like we are.

The smell is so closely attached to taste that it is difficult to know which one predominates in deciding food preference. A good cooking smell makes us hungry! Our dogs, however, have a much more developed smelling capacity (when compared to dogs, us humans are smell handicapped).

Different studies have allowed to know more about the subject: for dogs, smell seems crucial in order to detect food, but it isn't the only choice criteria. Texture and taste also have a role to play in this matter.

Our dog can be given food that smells like meat but that

doesn't contain any, or a mix of vegetables and meat (3/4 to 1/4 for example).

You think he will quickly discover his mistake! Try it. For me, it works with my bio kibbles.

14 SEXUALITY

The dog's sexual maturity occurs around the seventh month for males and between the seventh and the tenth month for females. But your dog might express sexual desires since the age of 7 weeks, in the form of games where intercourse is simulated. The female will be 'in heat', or have an estrus cycle, every six months. This interval may go from 4 to 8 months. These heat periods happen in spring and autumn; they mark the ovulation period and last around 15 to 20 days. Fecundation can happen between the 7th and the 14th day. The urine contains pheromones that attract males. The female can experience bleeding, which is called menstruation although the correct term is diapedesis; red cells go through the capillary walls. If a male shown his interest, the female will show her acceptance by placing her tail on the side, presenting her vagina.

During intercourse, there is a bulb on the dog's penis that will become engorged with blood. The male won't be able to get away from the female without releasing himself, and that could take 15 to 20 minutes. Do not try to separate them, whatever the reason, because that may cause the vagina to tear.

If you want two dogs to have intercourse, you should take the female to the male because males usually refuse to mate in unknown locations or when he's scared. You should note that the male is the only one to have a bone in his penis, called penile bone. There are cases of homosexuality in male dogs. This behavior is explained by sexual frustration. This frustration can cause hostility and fugues. Fugues, however, are less frequent in females, but they can become overexcited.

Many people still have trouble taking the decision of spaying their female dog. But if you are not aiming to have many dogs, this may be the best solution.

You shouldn't think of the spaying as an act of mutilation that will make your animal miserable. You should know that the behavior of a female depends on her instinct and hormones. The heat period happens twice a year, and last about 3 weeks. Apart from these two periods, you should know that your female dog has no desire for mating. And contrary to common beliefs, she doesn't need to have intercourse with a male at least once to be balanced.

You should know that contraception using injections or pills isn't the optimal solution, but it is effective.

The treatment will suppress the heat, but won't have an effect on the other hormonal problems caused by the presence of the ovaries, and that can sometimes cause illnesses. But in the wilderness, the female wolf isn't spayed. Surgical spaying is the removal of ovaries, with or without the uterus. This operation is very common and is done by all vets. Some veterinarians recommend to spay the female dog between the first and the second heat periods. Bull Terriers between the ages of 15 to 18 months, it is optimal, but check with your vet.

You can also opt for tubal ligation. But you should know

that this intervention doesn't suppress heat periods. Your female dog will not be able to have puppies, that's all.

Spaying increases the risk of weight gain. It is very important to pay attention to your female dog's nutrition the first 3 months after the operation and to make her exercise. You should know that a spayed female dog would probably live longer than normal dogs because she would have less health problems. Discuss it with your vet.

Today, there still are many people that refuse to neuter their dog, fearing that their animal would be miserable. You should know that the dog's behavior is closely linked to his instinct and hormones, and that he won't be miserable if he is neutered. If he never encounters a female in heat, a male dog will not feel the need to mate. So, contrary to popular beliefs, neutering won't disturb the dog's general balance.

The situation is far more complicated if he is stimulated by the presence of females, but no physical contact is made. The dog will then be overexcited and you will need a hormonal treatment to calm him. In addition, you should know that the dog would have many health issues if he is not neutered. But in the wilderness, the wolf is not neutered.

Neutering should be done between the ages of 10 to 12 months, before puberty.

The health issues encountered in non-neutered dogs would be centered around testicles and prostate:

A non-neutered dog becomes overexcited and has the tendency to run away during his heat periods. When in the presence of a female in heat, he will only listen to his sexual instinct and will ignore your orders. You should be careful, and at least use medical neutering especially during the risk periods.

Vasectomy is the ligation of the spermatic cords. That way,

the dog will still be able to have erections.

Personally, I am amazed by the speech of canine behaviorists who also are vets, and who preach the satisfaction of the dog's primary needs but recommend irreversible contraception. But let's face it, contraception is a 200-300 euros surgical act…

For my dogs, I usually go with reversible contraception, and I pay close attention during spring and autumn.

For my female dogs, temporary and reversible spaying uses synthetic hormones that stop ovulation and even heat periods. The used molecules usually are synthetic derivatives of progesterone (progestogen or gestagens). You have to use them in ano-estrous, to delay the appearance of estrous or in the beginning of pro estrous, to interrupt heat periods. Progestogens have a hormonal action that block the maturation phase of follicles and ovulation. The use of progestogens can have some complications. That's why you should, before using them for contraception, have great knowledge of the estrous cycle of the female dog, and conduct a preliminary medical examination to detect a pathology that may be a contraindication to the use of these molecules. You should be careful when using progestogens, especially with greyhounds.

For my male dogs, I use chemical neutering: implants of Deslorelin called SUPRELORIN. This product continuously releases hormones that chemically neuter the dog for 12 months. The dog is sterile 4 to 6 weeks after the implantation. Its effects are completely reversible. The implant is injected in the skin without general anesthesia and doesn't bother the dog. Many implants can be injected later.

I am not a vet, so I must insist that I am sharing my

experience. You have to read and discuss this subject, because a definitive contraception is an important choice.

Finally, I highlight the fact that I have selected dogs, LOFs, dogs that have passed aptitude tests with excellence, that are trained in canine sports, and that participate in beauty pageants two to three times a year.

I don't do dog breeding, but I accept reproduction according to the males and the females that I have. I have to so X-rays and DNA tests because I think it's a pity that great dogs that are compliant to standards and psychologically balanced do not participate in the maintaining of the race. But if you don't want to abide by the medical obligations imposed to breeders, you should choose definitive contraception.

But please, stop spreading false facts. Fugues, fights between males, domination behaviors can be easily handled with education and careful attention in mating seasons.

We should tell the truth: there are reasons other than those we've talked about, such as traffic, rivalry between particulars and professionals, economic interests of vets, the absence of follow-up and the increase of bastardy.

Breeding is a profession, it is regulated and protected. The majority of breeders are great professionals. You should know that breeders place dogs for free in selected families for reproduction purposes. Consanguinity should be controlled, and that genetic mixing is absolutely necessary to prevent genetic defects. Informed individuals and selected dogs working with breeders, that's a good thing. Wild reproduction is a real nuisance.

www.ingramcontent.com/pod-product-compliance
Lightning Source LLC
Chambersburg PA
CBHW040231240726
48664CB00001B/87